I0134727

It's Never too Late to Navigate

365 Quotes to a Better You

Compiled and Edited by

Melissa Eshleman

Original Edition

Find Your Way Publishing, Inc.
PO BOX 667
Norway, Maine

It's Never too Late to Navigate:
365 Quotes to a Better You

Copyright © 2013 Melissa Eshleman
Find Your Way Publishing paperback edition, 2013

Find Your Way Publishing, Inc.
PO BOX 667
Norway, ME 04268 U.S.A.
Orders at www.findyourwaypublishing.com

All rights reserved. **No part of this book may be reproduced, stored in a retrieval system or transmitted in any form or by any means, electronic, mechanical, photocopying, recording, or otherwise, without the written permission of the publisher.**

Find Your Way Publishing, Inc.
First Edition, 2013

ISBN-13: 978-0-9849322-3-8
ISBN-10: 0-9849322-3-2

Library of Congress Control Number: 2013943609

It's never too late to navigate /edited and compiled by Melissa Eshleman –
1st Ed

        p   cm
Includes index
        Summary A collection of quotations
        ISBN:978-0-9849322-3-8
        Quotations, English 2. Title: It's never too late to navigate
        3. Eshleman, Melissa

Printed in the United States of America.

Dedication

This book is dedicated to all who are growing and bettering themselves. To those who have learned to pick themselves up, dust themselves off, and continually move forward. And to those who are learning to appreciate and value this precious thing called 'Time'. It's never too late to move in the direction of your dreams. The time is now.

About this book

This book shares wisdom from some of history's greatest figures passed down over hundreds of years. It is meant to remind people of the strength that lies within to motivate, encourage and inspire them to stay positive and face life's challenges head on. This, in turn, increases an individual's capacity for personal growth, development and transformation.

As we move through life, we are either going forward, falling behind or remaining still. This book will help you to continue moving forward, giving you the inspiration you need to take on life's challenges and capture the opportunities presented to you. The quotes in this book help people find focus and clarity in their everyday lives.

It's Never too Late to Navigate: 365 Quotes to a Better You brings together the power of quotes and journaling, giving people the opportunity to write down their daily thoughts, goals and ideas. By doing so, they increase their ability to accomplish meaningful growth on a personal level. Rather than containing text-heavy tips and advice, the book aims to prompt creativity and self-reflection on the part of the reader through a simple and easy-to-use format.

Quotes have the power to create positive change. They can change your perspective, thereby open doors that beforehand appeared closed. Quotes are everywhere because they work. They motivate, encourage, and inspire. Quotes help people feel better when they feel down, depressed, or defeated. Quotes can generate strong emotions, instantly transform ones mood, and remind us that not only are we not alone, but that we are powerful warriors. That others before us have faced similar feelings and challenges and have persevered. Quotes remind us of our strength.

"I pick my favorite quotations and store them in my mind as ready armor, offensive or defensive, amid the struggle of this turbulent existence."

ROBERT BURNS

Quotes inspire, motivate, and remind us that we are capable. And by writing things down a part of your brain is triggered which increases your potential for growth, development, and transformation. Quotes open our minds, and writing things down stimulates our long-term memory, and is a key to effectiveness.

This book of quotes is simple and easy to use, yet effective. It is broken down by day with a small space to journal thoughts and actions that the quote may have conjured up or provoked. By bringing two powerful tools together; quotes and journaling, you will be creating and manifesting your own path with each new day.

This is your life, and you're creating it. Create the masterpiece that you desire. Move slowly in the direction that feels right to you. To get from point A to point B you need direction, a map if you will. You need to plan it out. Once you have a plan in place, you have to take many turns; many lefts and rights. You need to yield and stop often, many times unsure if you are going in the right direction. Although unsure at times, you keep moving forward. If you get off-track you simply learn from it, make a u-turn and get back on the correct path. Create a life map for yourself.

"People often say that this or that person has not yet found himself. But the self is not something one finds, it is something one creates."

THOMAS SZASZ

It's Never too Late to Navigate

365 Quotes to a Better You

"Finding oneself and one's path is like waking up on a foggy day. Be patient, and presently the fog will clear and that which has always been there can be seen. The path is already there to follow."

RASHEED OGUNLARU

1

"I've missed more than 900 shots in my career. I've lost almost 30 games. 26times, I've been trusted to take the game winning shot and missed. I've failed over and over and over again in my life. And that is why I succeed."

MICHAEL JORDAN

Thoughts/Actions:

2

"Everything can be taken from a man but one thing: the last of human freedoms - to choose one's attitude in any given set of circumstances, to choose one's own way."

VIKTOR E. FRANKL

Thoughts/Actions:

3

"A smooth sea never made a skillful sailor."

UNKNOWN

"You have to leave the city of your comfort and go into the wilderness of your intuition. What you'll discover will be wonderful. What you'll discover is yourself."

ALAN ALDA

Thoughts/Actions:

4

"Paying attention to what is true at every point along the way while you continue to hold your vision lets you make realistic decisions about which baby steps you will take to move yourself closer to your goal."

DAVID EMERALD

Baby steps will still get you to where you want to go. Just keep moving in the right direction.

Thoughts/Actions:

5

"Sometimes you win, sometimes you learn."

UNKNOWN

And learning is winning, so I guess it's always a win-win.

Thoughts/Actions:

6

"Only the weak are cruel. Gentleness can only be expected from the strong."

LEO BUSCAGLIA

Thoughts/Actions:

7

"The Mind: A beautiful servant, a dangerous master."

OSHO

Don't let your mind take you where ever IT wants to go... that's how negative thoughts creep in. Train your mind to work for you... positive thoughts lead to unlimited potential.

Thoughts/Actions:

8

"I am in competition with no one. I run my own race. I have no desire to play the game of being better than anyone, in any way, shape, or form. I just aim to improve, to be better than I was before. That's me and I'm free."

JENNY G. PERRY

Thoughts/Actions:

9

"Even if you are on the right track, you'll get run over if you just sit there."

WILL ROGERS

Thoughts/Actions:

10

"Someday, we'll forget the hurt, the reason we cried and who caused us pain. We will finally realize that the secret of being free is not revenge, but letting things unfold in their own way and own time. After all, what matters is not the first, but the last chapter of our life which shows how well we ran the race. So smile, laugh, forgive, believe and love all over again."

UNKNOWN

The secret of being free is to let things unfold in their own way and own time. In other words trust the Universe.

Thoughts/Actions:

11

"As I look back on my life, I realize that every time I thought I was being rejected from something good, I was actually being re-directed to something better."

STEVE MARABOLI

Just by looking at what appears to be a "bad" situation differently, can change it into something good.

Thoughts/Actions:

12

"Always pray to have eyes that see the best in people, a heart that forgives the worst, a mind that forgets the bad, and a soul that never loses faith in God."

UNKNOWN

See the best
Forgive the worst
Forget the bad
Always have faith

Thoughts/Actions:

13

"Every time you are tempted to react in the same old way, ask if you want to be a prisoner of the past or a pioneer of the future."

DEEPAK CHOPRA

Thoughts/Actions:

14

"Love all, trust a few, and do wrong to none."

WILLIAM SHAKESPEARE

Thoughts/Actions:

15

"A person's actions will tell you everything you need to know."

UNKNOWN

Thoughts/Actions:

16

"Focus on your blessings, not your misfortunes. Focus on your strengths, not your weaknesses. Relax and let life come to you... Try not to force anything."

UNKNOWN

Thoughts/Actions:

17

"Bless the broken road that let me straight to who I am today. A little bruised, a little battered but now stronger than ever."

UNKNOWN

Thoughts/Actions:

18

"I see my path, but I don't know where it leads. Not knowing where I'm going, is what inspires me to travel it..."

ROSALIA DE CASTRO

Thoughts/Actions:

19

"Pride is concerned with who is right. Humility is concerned with what is right."

EZRA T. BENSON

Thoughts/Actions:

20

"Never waste your time trying to explain who you are to people who are committed to misunderstanding you."

DREAM HAMPTON

Thoughts/Actions:

21

"I... recommend to every one of my Readers, the keeping a Journal of their Lives for one Week, and setting down punctually their whole Series of Employments during that Space of Time. This kind of Self-Examination would give them a true State of themselves, and incline them to consider seriously what they are about. One Day would rectify the Omissions of another, and make a Man weigh all those indifferent Actions, which, though they are easily forgotten, must certainly be accounted for."

JOSEPH ADDISON, 172

Thoughts/Actions:

22

"I am a slow walker, but I never walk backwards."

UNKNOWN

Thoughts/Actions:

23

"Through persistence, self-knowledge, prayer, commitment, optimism, a resolute trust in God and the building of your own personal moral strength, you can enjoy the blessings of a deeper faith and face the difficulties of life with courage and confidence."

NORMAN VINCENT PEALE

Thoughts/Actions:

24

"If you truly loved yourself, you could never hurt another."

BUDDHA

Thoughts/Actions:

25

"Do not pray for easy lives. Pray to be stronger men."

JOHN F KENNEDY

Thoughts/Actions:

26

"A loving person lives in a loving world. A hostile person lives in a hostile world. Everyone you meet is your mirror."

KEN KEYES

Thoughts/Actions:

27

"Greatness lies not in being strong, but in the right use of strength."

HENRY WARD BEECHER

Thoughts/Actions:

28

"The weaker are always anxious for justice and equality. The strong pay no heed to either."

ARISTOTLE

Thoughts/Actions:

29

"The weak can never forgive. Forgiveness is the attribute of the strong."

MAHATMA GANDHI

Thoughts/Actions:

30

"Failure will never overtake me if my determination to succeed is strong enough."

OG MANDINO

Thoughts/Actions:

31

"Great spirits have always encountered violent opposition from mediocre minds."

ALBERT EINSTEIN

Thoughts/Actions:

32

"A man must be big enough to admit his mistakes, smart enough to profit from them, and strong enough to correct them."

JOHN C. MAXWELL

Thoughts/Actions:

33

"He who conquers others is strong; He who conquers himself is mighty."

LAO TZU

Thoughts/Actions:

34

"He who believes is strong; he who doubts is weak. Strong convictions precede great actions."

LOUISA MAY ALCOTT

Thoughts/Actions:

35

"Set your sights high, the higher the better. Expect the most wonderful things to happen, not in the future but right now. Realize that nothing is too good. Allow absolutely nothing to hamper you or hold you up in any way."

EILEEN CADDY

Thoughts/Actions:

36

"You become a worrier by practicing worry. You can become free of worry by practicing the opposite and stronger habit of faith. With all the strength and perseverance you can command, start practicing faith."

NORMAN VINCENT PEALE

Thoughts/Actions:

37

"It is good to feel lost... because it proves you have a navigational sense of where "Home" is. You know that a place that feels like being found exists. And maybe your current location isn't that place but, Hallelujah, that unsettled, uneasy feeling of lost-ness just brought you closer to it."

ERIKA HARRIS

Thoughts/Actions:

38

"Keep looking my way, my head is held high. You want to bring me down? I dare you to try!"

UNKNOWN

Thoughts/Actions:

39

"In spiritual life there is no room for compromise. Awakening is not negotiable; we cannot bargain to hold on to things that please us while relinquishing things that do not matter to us. A lukewarm yearning for awakening is not enough to sustain us through the difficulties involved in letting go. It is important to understand that anything that can be lost was never truly ours; anything that we deeply cling to only imprisons us."

JACK KORNFIELD

Thoughts/Actions:

40

"As your faith is strengthened you will find that there is no longer the need to have a sense of control, that things will flow as they will, and that you will flow with them, to your great delight and benefit."

EMMANUEL TENEY

Thoughts/Actions:

41

"Emotions are great and wonderful things - they guide us, they enrich our experience in this world and others; they add to us in our understanding of ourselves. They serve us, motivate us and, propel us to advance in life and in living. I learn to trust my feelings and they have added to my self-trust in my judgments in situations, in people, in family, in lovers, in Spirit and I find it had never lead me wrong in anything. The only time it didn't work out was when I chose to ignore my feelings and went against myself."

ANGELICA VALERIO

Thoughts/Actions:

42

"Get excited about today! Rise in the morning with the spirit you knew in childhood. That spirit of eagerness, adventure, and certainty."

UNKNOWN

Thoughts/Actions:

43

"If your actions inspire others to dream more, learn more, do more and become more, you are a leader."

JOHN QUINCY ADAMS

Lead by example. Do good. Be good. Dream more. Learn more. Do more. Become more

"Great leaders don't tell you what to do... they show you how it's done."

GURU EDUARDO

Thoughts/Actions:

44

"You have within you right now, everything you need to deal with whatever the world can throw at you."

BRIAN TRACY

Thoughts/Actions:

45

"Behind me is infinite power. Before me is endless possibility. Around me is boundless opportunity. Why should I fear?"

UNKNOWN

Thoughts/Actions:

46

"A bird sitting on a tree is never afraid of the branch breaking because her trust is not in the branch but in her own wings."

UNKNOWN

Try not to worry... worry is a complete waste of time and steals your joy. Instead trust in your own wings. You've come this far. You've got this. You're strong. Believe it.

Thoughts/Actions:

47

"Everything comes to you in the right moment. Be patient."

UNKNOWN

Thoughts/Actions:

48

Make little changes in the right direction because "little by little, a little becomes A LOT"

TANZANIAN PROVERB

Thoughts/Actions:

49

"Sure sign of Spiritual Growth: What about me? Becomes... What can I do for you?"

MY RENEWED MIND

Thoughts/Actions:

50

"A wise woman who was traveling in the mountains found a precious stone in a stream. The next day she met another traveler who was hungry, and the wise woman opened her bag to share her food. The hungry traveler saw the precious stone and asked the woman to give it to him. She did so without hesitation. The traveler left, rejoicing in his good fortune. He knew the stone was worth enough to give him security for a lifetime. But a few days later he came back to return the stone to the wise woman."I've been thinking," He said, "I know how valuable the stone is, but I give it back in the hope that you can give me something even more precious. Give me what you have within you that enabled you to give me the stone."

UNKNOWN

Thoughts/Actions:

51

"One's mind, once stretched by a new idea, never regains its original dimensions."

OLIVER WENDELL HOLMES

Thoughts/Actions:

52

Ego Out = Wisdom In

If you want to reach bliss, let go of ego. The need to control... is only the ego. The need for approval... ego again. When you feel judgmental... it's just ego. Go beyond it. It's not who you are, and will only lower your vibration, attracting more of the same to you. Let it go. :)

"If you want to reach a state of bliss, then go beyond your ego and the internal dialogue. Make a decision to

relinquish the need to control, the need to be approved, and the need to judge. Those are the three things the ego is doing all the time. It's very important to be aware of them every time they come up."

DEEPAK CHOPRA

Thoughts/Actions:

53

"I will not let anyone walk through my mind with their dirty feet."

MAHATMA GANDHI

Keep your mind free of debris.

How? Change your mind. Think only thoughts that bring you joy! When you find yourself thinking thoughts that do not feel good or bring you joy, change your mind and think of something else. Would you rather be at the beach? Take a few minutes to visualize it. You have an imagination for a reason. Use it! The key is to use your mind to be happy NOW. :)

Keep your mind free of debris.

de·bris
noun \də-'brē
1. The scattered remains of something broken or destroyed; rubble or wreckage.
2. Something discarded: rubbish, trash, litter.

Thoughts/Actions:

54

"Life will break you. Nobody can protect you from that, and living alone won't either, for solitude will also break you with its yearning. You have to love. You have to feel. It is the reason you are here on Earth. You are here to risk your heart. You are here to be swallowed up. And when it happens that you are broken, or betrayed, or left, or hurt, or death brushes near, let yourself sit by an apple tree and listen to the apples falling all around you in heaps, wasting their sweetness. Tell yourself you tasted as many as you could."

LOUISE ERDRICH

Thoughts/Actions:

55

"Shallow men believe in luck. Strong men believe in cause and effect."

RALPH WALDO EMERSON

Thoughts/Actions:

56

"That strong mother doesn't tell her cub, Son, stay weak so the wolves can get you. She says, Toughen up, this is reality we are living in."

LAURYN HILL

Thoughts/Actions:

57

"The world breaks everyone, and afterward, some are strong at the broken places."

ERNEST HEMINGWAY

Thoughts/Actions:

58

"How far you go in life depends on your being tender with the young, compassionate with the aged, sympathetic with the striving and tolerant of the weak and strong. Because someday in your life you will have been all of these."

GEORGE WASHINGTON CARVER

Thoughts/Actions:

59

"Permanence, perseverance and persistence in spite of all obstacles, discouragements, and impossibilities: It is this, that in all things distinguishes the strong soul from the weak."

THOMAS CARLYLE

Thoughts/Actions:

60

"A strong positive mental attitude will create more miracles than any wonder drug."

PATRICIA NEAL

Thoughts/Actions:

61

"Don't wait for extraordinary opportunities. Seize common occasions and make them great. Weak men wait for opportunities; strong men make them."

ORISON SWETT MARDEN

Thoughts/Actions:

62

"In the world there is nothing more submissive and weak than water. Yet for attacking that which is hard and strong nothing can surpass it."

LAO TZU

Thoughts/Actions:

63

"A strong, successful man is not the victim of his environment. He creates favorable conditions. His own inherent force and energy compel things to turn out as he desires."

ORISON SWETT MARDEN

Thoughts/Actions:

64

"It's better to stumble along the way, than to give up completely... In the hope that you'll make it in the end.... no one said it would be easy, so every time you stumble and fall know that you'll be getting up stronger than before, with a God full of love and mercy, who's willing to forgive and forget your sins and give you a brand new start to move forward in the light. Through our pains, God brings growth."

UNKNOWN

Thoughts/Actions:

65

"Anyone can hide. Facing up to things, working through them, that's what makes you strong."

SARAH DESSEN

Thoughts/Actions:

66

"You have power over your mind - not outside events. Realize this, and you will find strength."

MARCUS AURELIUS

Thoughts/Actions:

67

"Some people believe holding on and hanging in there are signs of great strength. However, there are times when it takes much more strength to know when to let go and then do it."

ANN LANDERS

Thoughts/Actions:

68

"With the new day comes new strength and new thoughts."

ELEANOR ROOSEVELT

Thoughts/Actions:

69

"Although darkness may seem evident, don't despair, where there is dark there is always light. Just look up, even at night the moon shines bright, evidence that not all is bleak, although some nights it may seem, just remember these events are unforeseen. Mankind triumphs today in a society where the odds are stacked against them, survival diminishes daily as they strive to protect you and me."

MICHAEL SOTELO

Thoughts/Actions:

70

"Life is going to be tough. But I'm going to be tougher."

MARY GAOHLEE THAO

Thoughts/Actions:

71

"You don't always have to defend yourself with your words. Sometimes your silence gives people a clue that you have better thoughts in mind."

UNKNOWN

Thoughts/Actions:

72

"Never fear shadows, they simply mean there's a light shinning somewhere."

UNKNOWN

Thoughts/Actions:

73

"Strength does not come from physical capacity. It comes from an indomitable will."

MAHATMA GANDHI

Thoughts/Actions:

74

"Sooner or later our souls find their centre of gravity in a hot, salt-tasting kiss and a trembling touch. Trembling is a good sign: it means you're open to a world that knows you're coming."

LOUISE CAREY

Thoughts/Actions:

75

"Bottom line is, even if you see 'em coming, you're not ready for the big moments. No one asks for their life to change, not really. But it does. So what are we, helpless? Puppets? No. The big moments are gonna come. You can't help that. It's what you do afterwards that counts. That's when you find out who you are."

JOSS WHEDON

Thoughts/Actions:

76

"The strong person is not the good wrestler. Rather, the strong person is the one who controls himself when he is angry."

SAHIH AL-BUKHARI

Thoughts/Actions:

77

"Life doesn't get easier or more forgiving, we get stronger and more resilient."

STEVE MARABOLI

Thoughts/Actions:

78

"Though nothing can bring back the hour
Of splendor in the grass, of glory in the flower;
We will grieve not, rather find
Strength in what remains behind;
In the primal sympathy
Which having been must ever be..."

WILLIAM WORDSWORTH

Thoughts/Actions:

79

"Everything happens for a reason. People will push you around and take advantage of you so you eventually give up on everyone and trust nobody but yourself. Life isn't easy, but we all know that. These struggles that most of us all face is common throughout the world and we all got to learn that this only makes an individual stronger in the heart and mind. We have to accept that those nights of feeling lonely and stressed are nothing but ways to help push you into becoming a much better person. And that's what bids us a happy and wonderful life in the long run."

MARISA STEIN

Thoughts/Actions:

80

"One's dignity may be assaulted, vandalized and cruelly mocked, but it can never be taken away unless it is surrendered."

MICHAEL J. FOX

Thoughts/Actions:

81

"Grudges are for those who insist that they are owed something; forgiveness, however, is for those who are substantial enough to move on."

CRISS JAMI

Thoughts/Actions:

82

"And one has to understand that braveness is not the absence of fear but rather the strength to keep on going forward despite the fear."

PAULO COELHO

Thoughts/Actions:

83

"Life is filled with unanswered questions, but it is the courage to seek those answers that continues to give meaning to life. You can spend your life wallowing in despair, wondering why you were the one who was led towards the road strewn with pain, or you can be grateful that you are strong enough to survive it."

J.D. STROUBE

Thoughts/Actions:

84

"Why the hell have I been waiting for someone else to give me permission to summon all of my glorious self, to live my life? Find your spark. Create your venue. Cast yourself in the leading role of your life and find some others for supporting roles—and write your own script."

AGAPI STASSINOPOULOS

Thoughts/Actions:

85

"The secret to arriving at your destination is constant auto-correction in the face of the inevitable mistakes we all make. The error is not so much in getting off course. That part is inevitable. We're human. With auto-correction you can get off course and still reach your destination."

DR. LISSA RANKIN

Thoughts/Actions:

86

"I hope you live a life you're proud of. If you find that you're not, I hope you have the strength to start all over again."

ERIC ROTH

Thoughts/Actions:

87

"The weaker you are the louder you bark."

UNKNOWN

Thoughts/Actions:

88

"My attitude is that if you push me towards something that you think is a weakness, then I will turn that perceived weakness into a strength."

MICHAEL JORDAN

Thoughts/Actions:

89

"You can only let someone throw so many stones at you before you pick them all up, put them together and build a wall to keep them from doing it again!"

UNKNOWN

Thoughts/Actions:

90

"Risk anything! Care no more for the opinion of others ... Do the hardest thing on Earth for you. Act for yourself. Face the truth."

KATHERINE MANSFIELD

Thoughts/Actions:

91

"Strength isn't about bearing a cross of grief or shame. Strength comes from choosing your own path, and living with the consequences."

JENNIFER ARMINTROUT

Thoughts/Actions:

92

"Does anything in nature despair except man? An animal with a foot caught in a trap does not seem to despair. It is too busy trying to survive. It is all closed in, to a kind of still, intense waiting. Is this a key? Keep busy with survival. Imitate the trees. Learn to lose in order to recover, and remember that nothing stays the same for long, not even pain, psychic pain. Sit it out. Let it all pass. Let it go."

MAY SARTON

Thoughts/Actions:

93

"Give me strength, not to be better than my enemies, but to defeat my greatest enemy, the doubts within myself. Give me strength for a straight back and clear eyes, so when life fades, as the setting sun, my spirit may come to you without shame."

P.C. CAST

Thoughts/Actions:

94

"Self-pity is our worst enemy and if we yield to it, we can never do anything wise in this world."

HELEN KELLER

Thoughts/Actions:

95

"When your desires are strong enough you will appear to possess superhuman powers to achieve."

NAPOLEON HILL

Thoughts/Actions:

96

"To begin to think with purpose, is to enter the ranks of those strong ones who only recognize failure as one of the pathways to attainment."

JAMES ALLEN

Thoughts/Actions:

97

"Build up your weaknesses until they become your strong points."

KNUTE ROCKNE

Thoughts/Actions:

98

"Great occasions do not make heroes or cowards; they simply unveil them to the eyes of men. Silently and imperceptibly, as we wake or sleep, we grow strong or weak; and at last some crisis shows what we have become."

BROOKE FOSS WESTCOTT

Thoughts/Actions:

99

"It is the characteristic excellence of strong people that they can bring momentous issues to the fore and make a decision about them. The weak are always forced to decide between alternatives they have not chosen themselves."

DIETRICH BONHOEFFER

Thoughts/Actions:

100

"A failure establishes only this, that our determination to succeed was not strong enough."

CHRISTIAN NESTELL BOVEE

Thoughts/Actions:

101

"Be strong in body, clean in mind, lofty in ideals."

JAMES NAISMITH

Thoughts/Actions:

102

"The difference between perseverance and obstinacy is that one comes from a strong will, and the other from a strong won't."

HENRY WARD BEECHER

Thoughts/Actions:

103

"Always dream and shoot higher than you know you can do. Do not bother just to be better than your contemporaries or predecessors. Try to be better than yourself."

WILLIAM FAULKNER

Thoughts/Actions:

104

"The potential of the average person is like a huge ocean unsailed, a new continent unexplored, a world of possibilities waiting to be released and channeled toward some great good."

BRIAN TRACY

Thoughts/Actions:

105

"Once the soul awakens, the search begins and you can never go back. From then on, you are inflamed with a special longing that will never again let you linger in the lowlands of complacency and partial fulfillment.

The eternal makes you urgent. You are loath to let compromise or the threat of danger hold you back from striving toward the summit of fulfillment."

JOHN O'DONOHUE

Thoughts/Actions:

106

"All the strength and force of man comes from his faith in things unseen. He who believes is strong; he who doubts is weak."

JAMES FREEMAN CLARKE

Thoughts/Actions:

107

"The moment will arrive when you are comfortable with who you are, and what you are– bald or old or fat or poor, successful or struggling- when you don't feel the need to apologize for anything or to deny anything. To be comfortable in your own skin is the beginning of strength."

CHARLES B. HANDY

Thoughts/Actions:

108

"The Journey - One day you finally knew what you had to do, and began, though the voices around you kept shouting their bad advice -- though the whole house began to tremble and you felt the old tug at your ankles."Mend my life!" each voice cried. But you didn't stop. You knew what you had to do, though the wind pried with its stiff fingers at the very foundations, though their melancholy was terrible. It was already late enough, and a wild night, and the road full of fallen branches and stones. But little by little, as you left their voices behind, the stars began to burn through the sheets of clouds, and there was a new voice which you slowly recognized as your own, that kept you company as you strode deeper and deeper into the world, determined to do the only thing you could do -- determined to save the only life you could save."

MARY OLIVER

Thoughts/Actions:

109

"What does it mean if I'm afraid? Does it mean something bad is going to happen? No, it doesn't mean something bad is going to happen. It just means that you have the chance to be brave."

C. JOYBELL C.

Thoughts/Actions:

110

"Do not dilute the truth of your potential. We often convince ourselves that we cannot change, that we cannot overcome the circumstances of our lives. That is simply not true. You have been blessed with immeasurable power to make positive changes in your life. But you can't just wish it, you can't just hope it, you can't just want it... you have to LIVE it, BE it, DO it."

STEVE MARABOLI

Thoughts/Actions:

111

"It isn't where you came from; it's where you're going that counts."

ELLA FITZGERALD

Thoughts/Actions:

112

"We either make ourselves miserable, or we make ourselves strong. The amount of work is the same."

CARLOS CASTENADA

Thoughts/Actions:

113

"Strong people make as many mistakes as weak people. Difference is that strong people admit their mistakes, laugh at them, learn from them. That is how they become strong."

RICHARD J. NEEDHAM

Thoughts/Actions:

114

"The block of granite which was an obstacle in the pathway of the weak, became a stepping-stone in the pathway of the strong."

THOMAS CARLYLE

Thoughts/Actions:

115

"If people have a basic understanding of right from wrong, possess a strong desire to better themselves and persist in their cause, they can break the chain of any negative environment."

DAVE PELZER

Thoughts/Actions:

116

"Fire is the test of gold; adversity, of strong men."

MARTHA GRAHAM

Thoughts/Actions:

117

"The Divine wisdom has given us prayer, not as a means whereby to obtain the good things of Earth, but as a means whereby we learn to do without them; not as a means whereby we escape evil, but as a means whereby we become strong to meet it."

FREDERICK WILLIAM ROBERTSON

Thoughts/Actions:

118

"Anyone can give up; it is the easiest thing in the world to do. But to hold it together when everyone would expect you to fall apart, now that is true strength."

CHRIS BRADFORD

Thoughts/Actions:

119

"The law of evolution is that the strongest survives!' 'Yes, and the strongest, in the existence of any social species, are those who are most social. In human terms, most ethical...There is no strength to be gained from hurting one another. Only weakness."

URSULA K. LE GUIN

Thoughts/Actions:

120

"Strength of character means the ability to overcome resentment against others, to hide hurt feelings, and to forgive quickly."

LAWRENCE G. LOVASIK

Thoughts/Actions:

121

"Through humor, you can soften some of the worst blows that life delivers. And once you find laughter, no matter how painful your situation might be, you can survive it."

BILL COSBY

Thoughts/Actions:

122

"I know I have but the body of a weak and feeble woman, but I have the heart and stomach of a king, and of a king of England too."

ELIZABETH I TUDOR

Thoughts/Actions:

123

"The times are chaotic. For me, I would hope that people look at and gain strength by it. With everything that I do, I hope that they see people struggling to live decent, moral lives in a completely chaotic world. They see how hard it is, how often they fail, and how they get up and keep trying. That, to me, is the most important message I'm ever going to tell."

JOSS WHEDON

Thoughts/Actions:

124

"The authentic self is the best part of a human being. It's the part of you that already cares, that is already passionate about evolution. When your authentic self miraculously awakens and becomes stronger than your ego, then you will truly begin to make a difference in this world. You will literally enter into a partnership with the creative principle."

ANDREW COHEN

Thoughts/Actions:

125

"The harder the conflict, the more glorious the triumph. What we obtain too cheap, we esteem too lightly; it is dearness only that gives everything its value. I love the man that can smile in trouble, that can gather strength from distress, and grow."

THOMAS PAINE

Thoughts/Actions:

126

"You must not be frightened if a sadness rises up before you larger than any you have ever seen; if a restiveness, like light and cloud shadows, passes over your hands and over all you do. You must think that something is happening with you, that life has not forgotten you, that it holds you in its hand; it will not let you fall. Why do you want to shut out of your life any uneasiness, any miseries, or any depressions? For after all, you do not know what work these conditions are doing inside you."

RAINER MARIA RILKE

Thoughts/Actions:

127

"If you have a past with which you feel dissatisfied, then forget it, now. Imagine a new story for your life and believe in it. Focus only on the moments when you achieved what you desired, and that strength will help you to get what you want."

PAULO COELHO

Thoughts/Actions:

128

"Each pain makes you more strong, each betrayal more intelligent, every disappointment more skillful & each experience more wise."

UNKNOWN

Thoughts/Actions:

129

"Every time you are tempted to react in the same old way, ask if you want to be a prisoner of the past or a pioneer of the future."

DEEPAK CHOPRA

Thoughts/Actions:

130

"May you have enough happiness to make you sweet, enough trials to make you strong, enough sorrow to keep you human enough hope to make you happy."

UNKNOWN

Thoughts/Actions:

131

"You must be strong now. You must never give up. And when people make you cry and you are afraid of the dark, don't forget the light is always there."

UNKNOWN

Thoughts/Actions:

132

"Strong men can always afford to be gentle. Only the weak are intent on "giving as good as they get."

ELBERT HUBBARD

Thoughts/Actions:

133

"Celebrate your success and stand strong when adversity hits, for when the storm clouds come in, the eagles soar while the small birds take cover."

UNKNOWN

Thoughts/Actions:

134

"I learned the hard way that I cannot always count on others to respect my feelings, even if I respect theirs. Being a good person doesn't guarantee that others will be good people, too. You only have control over yourself and how you choose to be as a person. As for others, you can only choose to accept them or walk away."

UNKNOWN

Thoughts/Actions:

135

"A silly idea is current that good people do not know what temptation means. This is an obvious lie. Only those who try to resist temptation know how strong it is.... A man who gives in to temptation after five minutes simply does not know what it would have been

like an hour later. That is why bad people, in one sense, know very little about badness. They have lived a sheltered life by always giving in."

C.S. LEWIS

Thoughts/Actions:

136

"I would rather have a big burden and a strong back, than a weak back and a caddy to carry life's luggage"

ELBERT HUBBARD

Thoughts/Actions:

137

"It's not enough to have a dream unless I'm willing to pursue it. It's not enough to know what's right unless I'm strong enough to do it. It's not enough to join the crowd, to be acknowledged and accepted. I must be true to my ideals, even if I'm excluded and rejected. It's not enough to learn the truth unless I also learn to live it. It's not enough to reach for love unless I care enough to give it."

UNKNOWN

Thoughts/Actions:

138

"Nonviolence is a weapon of the strong."

MAHATMA GANDHI

Thoughts/Actions:

139

"May your days be many and your troubles be few. May all God's blessings descend upon you. May peace be within you may your heart be strong. May you find what you're seeking wherever you roam."

IRISH BLESSINGS

Thoughts/Actions:

140

"One of the hardest decisions you'll ever face in life is choosing whether to walk away or try harder."

UNKNOWN

Thoughts/Actions:

141

"I'm no more a wonder than anyone. And that's what makes the world magical. Every baby's a seed of wonder - that gets watered or it doesn't."

DEAN KOONTZ

Thoughts/Actions:

142

"Nothing is permanent in this wicked world, not even our troubles."

CHARLIE CHAPLIN

Thoughts/Actions:

143

"You've been given the innate power to shape your life."

STEVE MARABOLI

Thoughts/Actions:

144

"Look, no matter where you live, the biggest defect we human beings have is our shortsightedness. We don't see what we could be. We should be looking at our potential, stretching ourselves into everything we can become. But if you're surrounded by people who say 'I want mine now,' you end up with a few people with everything and a military to keep the poor ones from rising up and stealing it."

MITCH ALBOM

Thoughts/Actions:

145

"There is no planet, sun, or star could hold you if you but knew what you are."

RALPH WALDO EMERSON

Thoughts/Actions:

146

"The generality of mankind is lazy. What distinguishes men of genuine achievement from the rest of us is not so much their intellectual powers and aptitudes as their curiosity, their energy, their fullest use of their potentialities. Nobody really knows how smart or talented he is until he finds the incentives to use himself to the fullest. God has given us more than we know what to do with."

SYDNEY J. HARRIS

Thoughts/Actions:

147

"Fear clogged human potential."

TOBA BETA

Thoughts/Actions:

148

"Sometimes we need to forget some people from our past, because of one simple reason. They simply don't belong in our future."

UNKNOWN

Thoughts/Actions:

149

"If the whole universe can be found in our own body and mind, this is where we need to make our inquires. We all have the answers within ourselves, we just have not got in touch with them yet. The potential of finding the truth within requires faith in ourselves."

AYYA KHEMA

Thoughts/Actions:

150

"If we fail to realize our full potential as human beings, we live more on an animalistic level. This is fine for dogs, cats, and chimpanzees but doesn't work quite so well for women and men. Without the capacity to freely shape our own lives, much as a sculptor might carve stone, we inevitably slip into negativity and depression."

H.E. DAVEY

Thoughts/Actions:

151

"Never be satisfied. Always strive to improve no matter how good you think you are."

UNKNOWN

Thoughts/Actions:

152

"When I look back on my life I can see the pain I've endured, the mistakes I've made and the hard times I've suffered. When I look in the mirror I see how strong I've become, the lessons I've learned and I'm proud of who I am."

DAVES WORDS OF WISDOM

Thoughts/Actions:

153

"Any intelligent fool can make things bigger, more complex, and more violent. It takes a touch of genius - and a lot of courage - to move in the opposite direction."

ALBERT EINSTEIN

Thoughts/Actions:

154

"If every 8 year old in the world is taught meditation, we will eliminate violence from the world within one generation."

DALAI LAMA

Thoughts/Actions:

155

"We lift ourselves by our thought, we climb upon our vision of ourselves. If you want to enlarge your life, you must first enlarge your thought of it and of yourself. Hold the ideal of yourself as you long to be, always, everywhere - your ideal of what you long to attain - the ideal of health, efficiency, success."

ORISON SWETT MARDEN

Thoughts/Actions:

156

"Finding your passion is about finding your authentic self. The one you've buried beneath other people's needs. The part of you that never gets old or tired."

LISA VILLA PROSEN

Thoughts/Actions:

157

"Life's challenges are not supposed to paralyze you, they're supposed to help you discover who you are."

BERNICE JOHNSON REAGON

Thoughts/Actions:

158

"If we could look into each other's hearts and understand the unique challenges each of us faces, I think we would treat each other much more gently, with more love, patience, tolerance, and care."

MARVIN J. ASTON

Thoughts/Actions:

159

"Being strong doesn't always mean you have to fight the battle. True strength is being adult enough to walk away from the nonsense with your head held high."

UNKNOWN

Thoughts/Actions:

160

"The only person you are destined to become is the person you decide to be."

RALPH WALDO EMERSON

Thoughts/Actions:

161

"There comes a moment in every life when the Universe presents you with an opportunity to rise to your potential. An open door that only requires the heart to walk through, seize it and hang on. The choice is never simple. It's never easy. It's not supposed to be. But those who travel this path have always looked back and realized that the test was always about the heart. ...The rest is just practice."

JAIME BUCKLEY, PRELUDE TO A HERO

Thoughts/Actions:

162

"Being happy is the cornerstone of all that you are! Nothing is more important than that you feel good! And you have absolute and utter control about that because you can choose the thought that makes you worry or the thought that makes you happy; the things that thrill you, or the things that worry you. You have the choice in every moment."

ABRAHAM HICKS

Thoughts/Actions:

163

"There are no choices that are really a detour that will take you far from where you're wanting to be -- because your Inner Being is always guiding you to the next, and the next, and the next. So don't be concerned that you may make a fatal choice, because there aren't any of those. You are always finding your balance. It's a never ending process."

ABRAHAM HICKS

Thoughts/Actions:

164

"Strong people don't put others down... They lift them up."

MICHAEL P. WATSON

Thoughts/Actions:

165

"The foundation stones for a balanced success are honesty, character, integrity, faith, love, and loyalty."

ZIG ZIGLAR

Thoughts/Actions:

166

"The tongue has no bones, but is strong enough to break a heart. So be careful with your words."

VERYBESTQUOTES.COM

Thoughts/Actions:

167

"Sometimes you have to run from the people you love, not for the sake of letting them realize your worth, but for you to realize your own..."

UNKNOWN

Thoughts/Actions:

168

"Entire water of the sea can't sink a ship unless it gets inside the ship. Similarly, negativity of the world can't put you down unless you allow it to get inside you."

UNKNOWN

Thoughts/Actions:

169

"We are human. We are not perfect. We are alive. We try things. We make mistakes. We stumble. We fall. We get hurt. We rise again. We try again. We keep learning. We keep growing. And... we are thankful for this priceless opportunity called life."

UNKNOWN

Thoughts/Actions:

170

"You teach people how to treat you. By what you allow, what you stop, and what you reinforce."

TONY GASKINS

Thoughts/Actions:

171

"If you always put limits on everything you do, physical or anything else. It will spread into your work and into your life. There are no limits. There are only plateaus, and you must not stay there, you must go beyond them."

BRUCE LEE

Thoughts/Actions:

172

"If you continuously compete with others, you become bitter. But if you continuously compete with yourself, you become better."

UNKNOWN

Thoughts/Actions:

173

"Always end the day with a positive thought. No matter how hard things were, tomorrow is a fresh opportunity to make it better."

UNKNOWN

Thoughts/Actions:

174

Top 10 Words of Wisdom from Gandhi

1. Be the change.
2. What you think you become.
3. Where there is love there is life.
4. Learn as if you'll live forever.
5. Your health is your real wealth.
6. Have a sense of humor.
7. Your life is your message.
8. Action expresses priorities.
9. Our greatness is being able to remake ourselves.
10. Find yourself in the service of others.

Thoughts/Actions:

175

"Forgiveness does not always lead to a healed relationship. Some people are not capable of love, and it might be wise to let them go along with your anger. Just wish them well and take care of yourself."

UNKNOWN

Thoughts/Actions:

176

"Respect yourself enough to walk away from anything that no longer serves you, grows you, or makes you happy."

UNKNOWN

Thoughts/Actions:

177

"Great minds discuss ideas. Average minds discuss events. Small minds discuss people."

ELEANOR ROOSEVELT

Thoughts/Actions:

178

"It never gets easier. You just get stronger and better."

UNKNOWN

Thoughts/Actions:

179

"Thoughts are boomerangs, returning with precision to their source. Choose wisely which ones you throw."

UNKNOWN

Thoughts/Actions:

180

"If you don't like something in your life, change it. If you can't change it, change the way you think about it!"

UNKNOWN

Thoughts/Actions:

181

"It's not about restrictions. It's about creating new habits."

UNKNOWN

Thoughts/Actions:

182

"The primary cause of unhappiness is never the situation but your thoughts about it. Be aware of the thoughts you are thinking. Separate them from the situation, which is always neutral. It is as it is."

ECKHART TOLLE

Thoughts/Actions:

183

"Don't be too hard on yourself. There are plenty of people willing to do that for you. Love yourself and be proud of everything that you do. Even mistakes mean you're in the game and at least you're trying."

UNKNOWN

Thoughts/Actions:

184

"Life isn't meant to be easy, it's meant to be LIVED. Sometimes good, other times rough. But with every up and down, you learn lessons that make you STRONG."

UNKNOWN

Thoughts/Actions:

185

"If you have a problem with me, give me a call. If you don't have my number then that means you don't know me well enough to have a problem."

UNKNOWN

Thoughts/Actions:

186

"Small daily improvements are the key to staggering long-term results."

UNKNOWN

Thoughts/Actions:

187

"The ones who say "you can't" and "you won't" are probably the ones scared that "you will".

UNKNOWN

Thoughts/Actions:

188

"If you carry the bricks from your past relationship, you will end up building the same house."

UNKNOWN

Thoughts/Actions:

189

"If you don't build YOUR dream, someone will hire you to help build theirs."

TONY GASKINS

Thoughts/Actions:

190

"In this house we do real. We do mistakes. We do I'm sorry. We do fun. We do hugs. We do second chances. We do Happy. We do forgiveness. We do really loud. We do family. We do love."

UNKNOWN

Thoughts/Actions:

191

How to Begin Rebuilding Life from Within

Love yourself, unconditionally.
Release your bottled up emotions.
Make time for long walks, alone.
Avoid living beyond your means.
Nurture your inner strength.
Stop apologizing for being you.
Surround yourself with positive people.
Embrace your situation, whatever it may be.

UNKNOWN

Thoughts/Actions:

192

"Sometimes you need to step outside, get some air, and remind yourself of who you are and who you want to be."

UNKNOWN

Thoughts/Actions:

193

"Peace is the result of retraining your mind to process life as it is, rather than as you think it should be."

WAYNE DYER

Thoughts/Actions:

194

Top 5 Regrets of the Dying

I wish I had the courage to live a life true to myself, not the life others expected of me.
I wish I hadn't worked so hard.
I wish I had the courage to express my feelings.
I wish I had stayed in touch with my friends.
I wish I had let myself be happy.

Thoughts/Actions:

195

"Take your attention away from what you don't want and all the emotional charge around it, and place your attention on what you wish to experience."

MICHAEL BERNARD BECKWITH

Thoughts/Actions:

196

"The price of anything is the amount of life you exchange for it."

HENRY DAVID THOREAU

Thoughts/Actions:

197

"Life is meant to be a challenge, because challenges are what make you grow."

MANNY PACQUIAO

Thoughts/Actions:

198

"Move out of your comfort zone. You can only grow if you are willing to feel awkward and uncomfortable when you try something new."

BRIAN TRACY

Thoughts/Actions:

199

"Effort only fully releases its reward after a person refuses to quit."

UNKNOWN

Thoughts/Actions:

200

"Every test in our life makes us bitter or better, every problem comes to break us or make us. The choice is ours whether we become VICTIM or VICTOR."

UNKNOWN

Thoughts/Actions:

201

"I'm not in this world to live up to your expectations and you're not in this world to live up to mine."

BRUCE LEE

Thoughts/Actions:

202

"I've failed over and over again in my life and that is why I succeed."

MICHAEL JORDAN

Thoughts/Actions:

203

"What do I fear?
I fear stagnation and lack of progress.
I fear never reaching my potential and being average.
I fear being forgotten...The past...Yesterday's news.
I fear giving up and being passed by, going softly into that good night.
I fear settling, giving in to the mediocrity.
I fear not feeling these fears anymore and just floating along.
These fears feed me, they nourish me, they drive me.
I love my fear."

UNKNOWN

Thoughts/Actions:

204

"Impossible is just a big word thrown around by small men who find it easier to live in the world they've been given than to explore the power they have to change it. Impossible is not a fact. It's an opinion. Impossible is not a declaration. It's a dare. Impossible is potential. Impossible is temporary. Impossible is nothing."

MUHAMMAD ALI

Thoughts/Actions:

205

"Do today what others won't, so tomorrow you can do what others can't."

JERRY RICE

Thoughts/Actions:

206

"The extra mile is the stretch of road that is never crowded."

UNKNOWN

Thoughts/Actions:

207

"Know your limitations and then defy them."

UNKNOWN

Thoughts/Actions:

208

"I hated every minute of training, but I said, 'Don't quit. Suffer now and live the rest of your life as a Champion!' "

MUHAMMAD ALI

Thoughts/Actions:

209

"Nothing can stop the man with the right mental attitude from achieving his goal; nothing on Earth can help the man with the wrong attitude."

THOMAS JEFFERSON

Thoughts/Actions:

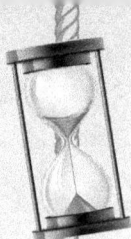

210

"Some people think that to be strong is to never feel pain. In reality, the strongest people are the ones who feel it, understand it, and accept it."

UNKNOWN

Thoughts/Actions:

211

"You can have results or excuses, but not both."

UNKNOWN

Thoughts/Actions:

212

"Our greatest glory is not in never falling, but in rising every time we fall."

CONFUCIUS

Thoughts/Actions:

213

"Strength doesn't come from what you can do. It comes from overcoming the things you once thought you couldn't."

UNKNOWN

Thoughts/Actions:

214

"Do not pray for an easy life, pray for the strength to endure a difficult one."

BRUCE LEE

Thoughts/Actions:

215

"I'm not out there sweating for 3 hours every day just to find out what it feels like to sweat."

MICHAEL JORDAN

Thoughts/Actions:

216

"We cannot solve our problems with the same thinking we used when we created them."

ALBERT EINSTEIN

Thoughts/Actions:

217

"Why do I succeed?
I succeed because I am willing to do things you are not.
I will fight against the odds.
I will sacrifice.
I am not shackled by fear, insecurity or doubt.
I feel those emotions - drink them in and then swallow them away to the blackness of hell.
I am motivated by accomplishment, not pride.
Pride consumes the weak - kills their heart from within.
If I fall - I will get up.
If I am beaten - I will return.
I will never stop getting better.
I will never give up - ever.
That is why I succeed."

UNKNOWN

Thoughts/Actions:

218

"We are what we repeatedly do. Excellence then is not an act, but a habit."

ARISTOTLE

Thoughts/Actions:

219

"Before success comes in any man's life, he's sure to meet with much temporary defeat and, perhaps some failures. When defeat overtakes a man, the easiest and the most logical thing to do is to quit. That's exactly what the majority of men do."

NAPOLEON HILL

Thoughts/Actions:

220

"Our lives are not determined by what happens to us but by how we react to what happens, not by what life brings to us, but by the attitude we bring to life. A positive attitude causes a chain reaction of positive thoughts, events, and outcomes. It is a catalyst; a spark that creates extraordinary results."

UNKNOWN

Thoughts/Actions:

221

"It is not the critic who counts; not the man who points out how the strong man stumbles, or where the doer of deeds could have done them better. The credit belongs to the man who is actually in the arena, whose face is marred by dust and sweat and blood, who strives valiantly; who errs and comes short again and again; because there is not effort without error and shortcomings; but who does actually strive to do the deed; who knows the great enthusiasm, the great devotion, who spends himself in a worthy cause, who at the best knows in the end the triumph of high achievement and who at the worst, if he fails, at least he fails while daring greatly. So that his place shall never be with those cold and timid souls who know neither victory nor defeat."

THEODORE ROOSEVELT

Thoughts/Actions:

222

"Whatever it is you choose to do, do it safely, but do it. Don't be afraid to live, rather be afraid to die old and have done nothing."

UNKNOWN

Thoughts/Actions:

223

"Adversity introduces us to ourselves."

JOSEFA ILOILO

Thoughts/Actions:

224

"Hatred is the coward's answer for being intimidated."

GEORGE BERNARD SHAW

Thoughts/Actions:

225

"Familiarity breeds contempt, while rarity wins admiration."

APULEIUS

Thoughts/Actions:

226

"Unless you try to do something beyond what you have already mastered, you will never grow."

RONALD OSBORN

Thoughts/Actions:

227

"Twenty years from now you will be more disappointed by the things you didn't do than by the ones you did do. So throw off the bowlines. Sail away from the safe harbor. Catch the trade winds in your sails. Explore. Dream. Discover."

MARK TWAIN

Thoughts/Actions:

228

"If you want something you never had, you have to do something you never did."

UNKNOWN

Thoughts/Actions:

229

"Only those who will risk going too far can possibly find out how far one can go."

T.S. ELIOT

Thoughts/Actions:

230

"Never, never, never give up!"

WINSTON CHURCHILL

Thoughts/Actions:

231

"Vague goals beget vague methods; the unfocused mind is the vulnerable mind, deeply susceptible to nonsense."

DANIEL DUANE

Thoughts/Actions:

232

"Security is mostly a superstition. It does not exist in nature, nor do the children of men as a whole experience it. Avoiding danger is no safer in the long run than outright exposure. Life is either a daring adventure, or nothing."

HELEN KELLER

Thoughts/Actions:

233

"We get attached to having a future. And thinking that we might not have a future past the next day is a really interesting mental trip to go down. It really illuminates for me what's important."

STEVE HOUSE

Thoughts/Actions:

234

"We are a nation of physical animals who have forgotten how much we enjoy being that. We are cushioned by this kind of make-believe, unreal world and have no idea what we can survive because we are never challenged or tested."

CHUCK PALAHNIUK

Thoughts/Actions:

235

"What kind of man makes it through Hell Week? That's hard to say. But I do know—generally—who won't make it. There are a dozen types that fail: the

weight-lifting meatheads who think that the size of their biceps is an indication of their strength, the kids covered in tattoos announcing to the world how tough they are, the preening leaders who don't want to get dirty, and the look-at-me former athletes who have always been told they are stars but have never have been pushed beyond the envelope of their talent to the core of their character. In short, those who fail are the ones who focus on show. The vicious beauty of Hell Week is that you either survive or fail, you endure or you quit, you do—or you do not.

Some men who seemed impossibly weak at the beginning of SEAL training—men who puked on runs and had trouble with pull-ups—made it. Some men who were skinny and short and whose teeth chattered just looking at the ocean also made it. Some men, who were visibly afraid, sometimes to the point of shaking, made it too. Almost all the men who survived possessed one common quality. Even in great pain, faced with the test of their lives, they had the ability to step outside of their own pain, put aside their own fear and ask: How can I help the guy next to me? They had more than the "fist" of courage and physical strength. They also had a heart large enough to think about others, to dedicate themselves to a higher purpose."

LT. CMDR. GREITENS TALKING ABOUT THE QUALITIES OF THE US NAVY SEALS

Thoughts/Actions:

236

"To dream anything that you want to dream.
That's the beauty of the human mind.
To do anything that you want to do.
That is the strength of the human will.
To trust yourself to test your limits.
That is the courage to succeed."

BERNARD EDMONDS

Thoughts/Actions:

237

"Groundbreaking innovators generate and execute far more ideas."

FRANS JOHANSSON

Thoughts/Actions:

238

"Reduce everything you want to do, to an action you can do right now."

JASON RANDAL

Thoughts/Actions:

239

"Don't be a victim, don't be a perpetrator and above all don't be a bystander."

UNKNOWN

Thoughts/Actions:

240

"Pain is inevitable; suffering is optional."

DALAI LAMA

Thoughts/Actions:

241

"So we shall let the reader answer this question for himself: Who is the happier man, he who has braved the storm of life and lived, or he who has stayed securely on shore and merely existed?"

HUNTER S. THOMPSON

Thoughts/Actions:

242

"Adventure is worthwhile."

ARISTOTLE

Thoughts/Actions:

243

"When a child has a dream and a parent says, "It's not financially feasible; you can't make a living at that; don't do it," we say to the child, run away from home... You must follow your dream. You will never be joyful if you don't. Your dream may change, but you've got to stay after your dreams. You have to.""

ABRAHAM HICKS

Thoughts/Actions:

244

"There is nothing sadder in this world than the waste of human potential. The purpose of evolution is to raise us out of the mud, not have us groveling in it"

ANDREW SCHNEIDER

Thoughts/Actions:

245

"The victim mindset dilutes the human potential. By not accepting personal responsibility for our circumstances, we greatly reduce our power to change them."

STEVE MARABOLI

Thoughts/Actions:

246

"Understand: people will constantly attack you in life. One of their main weapons will be to instill in you doubts about yourself – your worth, your abilities, your potential. They will often disguise this as their objective opinion, but invariably it has a political purpose – they want to keep you down."

ROBERT GREENE

Thoughts/Actions:

247

"From a mind filled with infinite love comes the power to create infinite possibilities. We have the power to think in ways that reflect and attract all the love in the world. Such thinking is called enlightenment. Enlightenment is not a process we work toward, but a choice available to us in any instant."

MARIANNE WILLIAMSON

Thoughts/Actions:

248

"You are a creator; you create with your every thought. You often create by default, for you are getting what you are giving your attention to wanted or unwanted but you know by how it feels if what you are getting (creating) is what you are wanting or if it is not what you are wanting. Where is your attention focused?"

ABRAHAM HICKS

Thoughts/Actions:

249

"Most humans, in varying degrees, are already dead. In one way or another they have lost their dreams, their ambitions, their desire for a better life. They have surrendered their fight for self-esteem and they have

compromised their great potential. They have settled for a life of mediocrity, days of despair and nights of tears. They are no more than living deaths confined to cemeteries of their choice. Yet they need not remain in that state. They can be resurrected from their sorry condition. They can each perform the greatest miracle in the world. They can each come back from the dead..."

OG MANDINO

Thoughts/Actions:

250

"People who repeatedly attack your confidence and self-esteem are quite aware of your potential, even if you are not."

WAYNE GERARD TROTMAN

Thoughts/Actions:

251

We are given the potential to excel, whether we do or not is entirely up to us."

STEVEN REDHEAD

Thoughts/Actions:

252

"Every day that we fail to live out the maximum of our potentialities we kill the Shakespeare, Dante, Homer, Christ which is in us."

HENRY MILLER

Thoughts/Actions:

253

"Nobody ever talks about the pyramids that weren't built, the books that weren't written, the songs that weren't sung. Stop letting your fear condemn you to mediocrity. Get out of your own way. Your dreams are a poetic reflection of your soul's wishes. Be courageous enough to follow them. There is no greater time than now to experience the full power of your potential. Make this the day you take the first step in the beautiful journey of bringing your dreams to life."

STEVE MARABOLI

Thoughts/Actions:

254

"You must decide if you are going to rob the world or bless it with the rich, valuable, potent, untapped resources locked away within you."

MYLES MUNROE

Thoughts/Actions:

255

"There exists in man a mass of sense lying in a dormant state, and which, unless something excites it to action, will descend with him, in that condition, to the grave."

THOMAS PAINE

Thoughts/Actions:

256

"If you are ending up where you want to be, what difference does it make whether you went fast or slow? Or what difference does it make whether it was painful before it got really good? Isn't that the point of free will? You get to choose."

ABRAHAM HICKS

Thoughts/Actions:

257

"Sometimes I've believed as many as six impossible things before breakfast."

LEWIS CARROLL

Thoughts/Actions:

258

"What we can or cannot do, what we consider possible or impossible, is rarely a function of our true capability. It is more likely a function of our beliefs about who we are."

ANTHONY ROBBINS

Thoughts/Actions:

259

"Believe and act as if it were impossible to fail."

CHARLES F. KETTERING

Thoughts/Actions:

260

"If you just set out to be liked, you would be prepared to compromise on anything at any time, and you would achieve nothing."

MARGARET THATCHER

Thoughts/Actions:

261

"Go without a coat when it's cold; find out what cold is. Go hungry; keep your existence lean. Wear away the fat, get down to the lean tissue and see what it's all about. The only time you define your character is when you go without. In times of hardship, you find out what you're made of and what you're capable of. If you're never tested, you'll never define your character."

HENRY ROLLINS

Thoughts/Actions:

262

"When I lost my possessions, I found my creativity."

YIP HARBURG

Thoughts/Actions:

263

"When I'm sad, I stop being sad and be awesome instead. True story."

BARNEY STINSON

Thoughts/Actions:

264

"You let people stick a finger in your face and tell you you're no good. And when things got hard, you started looking for something to blame, like a big shadow. Let me tell you something you already know. The world ain't all sunshine and rainbows. It's a very mean and nasty place and I don't care how tough you are it will beat you to your knees and keep you there permanently if you let it. You, me, or nobody is gonna hit as hard as life. But it ain't about how hard ya hit. It's about how hard you can get it and keep moving forward. How much you can take and keep moving forward. That's how winning is done! Now if you know what you're worth then go out and get what you're worth. But ya gotta be willing to take the hits, and not pointing fingers saying you ain't where you wanna be because of him, or her, or anybody! Cowards do that and that ain't you! You're better than that!"

ROCKY BALBOA

Thoughts/Actions:

265

"You know, I looked at my face in the mirror this morning, and I like being old. My face has more content and when I train in the gym now, I am not training to be strong or handsome - just better than I was yesterday. These days the race is just against myself."

JEAN CLAUDE VAN DAMME

Thoughts/Actions:

266

"Disciplining yourself to do what you know is right and important, although difficult, is the highroad to pride, self-esteem, and personal satisfaction."

MARGARET THATCHER

Thoughts/Actions:

267

"Age is not measured by years. Nature does not equally distribute energy. Some people are born old and tired while others are going strong at seventy."

DOROTHY THOMPSON

Thoughts/Actions:

268

"My strong point, if I have a strong point, is performance. I always do more than I say. I always produce more than I promise."

RICHARD M. NIXON

Thoughts/Actions:

269

"To hell with circumstances, I create opportunities."

BRUCE LEE

Thoughts/Actions:

270

"You're picky about the car you drive. You're picky about what you wear. You're picky about what you put in your mouth. We want you to be pickier about what you think."

ABRAHAM HICKS

Thoughts/Actions:

271

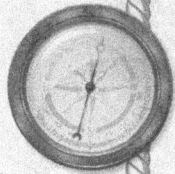

"The hardest thing in the world is to simplify your life. It's so easy to make it complex. Solution may be for a lot of the world's problems is to turn around and take a forward step. You can't just keep trying to make a flawed system work."

YVON CHOUINARD

Thoughts/Actions:

272

"The free soul is rare, but you know it when you see it. Basically because you feel good, very good when you are near them."

CHARLES BUKOWSKI

Thoughts/Actions:

273

"You can discover more about a person in an hour of play than in a year of conversation."

PLATO

Thoughts/Actions:

274

"This is your life. Do what you love, and do it often.
If you don't like something, change it.
If you don't like your job, quit.
If you don't have enough time, stop watching TV.
If you are looking for the love of your life, stop;
They will be waiting for you when you start doing things you love.
Stop over analyzing, life is simple.
All emotions are beautiful.
When you eat, appreciate every last bite.
Open your mind, arms, and heart to new things and people, we are united in our differences.
Ask the next person you see what their passion is, and share your inspiring dream with them.
Travel often; getting lost will help you find yourself.
Some opportunities only come once, seize them.
Life is about the people you meet, and the things that you create with them so go out and start creating.
Life is short.
Live your dream and share your passion."

THE HOLSTEE MANIFESTO

Thoughts/Actions:

275

"Give me six hours to chop down a tree and I'll spend four sharpening my axe."

ABRAHAM LINCOLN

Thoughts/Actions:

276

"Finding the center of strength within ourselves is in the long run the best contribution we can make to our fellow men. ... One person with indigenous inner strength exercises a great calming effect on panic among people around him. This is what our society needs — not new ideas and inventions; important as these are, and not geniuses and supermen, but persons who can "be", that is, persons who have a center of strength within themselves."

ROLLO MAY, MAN'S SEARCH FOR HIMSELF

Thoughts/Actions:

277

"If you doubt you can accomplish something, then you can't accomplish it. You have to have confidence in your ability, and then be tough enough to follow through."

ROSALYNN CARTER

Thoughts/Actions:

278

"One way of giving yourself a strong incentive to reach your goal is to commit to pay money to someone if you fail. Better yet, you can specify that you will have to pay a certain sum to a cause that you detest."

PETER SINGER

Thoughts/Actions:

279

"If we feel inwardly strong, we will have no need or desire to speak ill of others."

SRI CHINMOY

Thoughts/Actions:

280

"Always think extra hard before crossing over to a bad side, if you were weak enough to cross over, you may not be strong enough to cross back!"

VICTORIA ADDINO

Thoughts/Actions:

281

"Weak people believe what is forced on them. Strong people what they wish to believe, forcing that to be real."

GENE WOLFE

Thoughts/Actions:

282

"The path of peace is not a passive journey. It takes incredible strength not to open a can of 'whoop-ass', justifiably, when ones button is pushed."

T.F. HODGE

Thoughts/Actions:

283

"Focus on your goal, but do not lose sight of this moment. Feel happy and grateful for every moment on the journey to your goal."

JENNIFER GAYLE

Thoughts/Actions:

284

"The only way to eliminate darkness is to turn on a light."

UNKNOWN

Thoughts/Actions:

285

"I don't have time" is the grown-up version of "The dog ate my homework."

UNKNOWN

Thoughts/Actions:

286

"The most common way people give up their power is by thinking they don't have any."

UNKNOWN

Thoughts/Actions:

287

"No one can prepare you for what heights you will soar until you spread your wings."

UNKNOWN

Thoughts/Actions:

288

15 Things To Give Up...

1. Doubting yourself
2. Negative thinking
3. Fear of failure
4. Destructive relationships
5. Gossiping
6. Criticizing yourself or others
7. Anger
8. Comfort eating
9. Laziness
10. Negative self talk
11. Procrastination
12. Fear of success
13. Anything excessive
14. People pleasing
15. Putting others needs before your own.

UNKNOWN

Thoughts/Actions:

289

"Surround yourself with the dreamers and the doers, the believers and the thinkers, but most of all; surround yourself with those who see the greatness within you even when you don't see it yourself."

EDMUND LEE

Thoughts/Actions:

290

"I choose to live by choice, not by chance; to make changes, not excuses; to be motivated and not manipulated; to be useful, not used. I choose self-esteem, not self-pity; to listen to my inner voice, not the random opinions of others."

UNKNOWN

Thoughts/Actions:

291

"Moving from a Victim to Creator is a fundamental shift of mind."

DAVID EMERALD

Thoughts/Actions:

292

"A man can be judged by his past; however, it's his future that will define him."

DANIEL JOHNSON

Thoughts/Actions:

293

"The best thing about life is that nothing is written in stone. You can change your story any time you choose."

JENNIFER GAYLE

Thoughts/Actions:

294

"Every King was once a crying baby. And every building was once a picture. It's not about where you are today, but where you will reach tomorrow."

UNKNOWN

Thoughts/Actions:

295

"You will never change your life until you change something you do daily."

UNKNOWN

Thoughts/Actions:

296

"Keep away from people who try to belittle your ambitions. Small people always do that, but the really great make you feel that you, too, can become great."

MARK TWAIN

Thoughts/Actions:

297

"If you're still looking for that one person who can change your life, take a look in the mirror."

ROMAN PRICE

Thoughts/Actions:

298

"Never be afraid to change your vision, set new goals, and challenge yourself. Life is best experienced without boundaries."

CYLE PARKER

Thoughts/Actions:

299

"Without a plan you're going to stay where you are. It's time to make a move."

THEMA DAVIS

Thoughts/Actions:

300

"People know you for the great things you've done, not for the great things you planned to do."

UNKNOWN

Thoughts/Actions:

301

"You will never find time for anything. You must make it."

CHARLES BUXTON

Thoughts/Actions:

302

"Big things often have small beginnings."

UNKNOWN

Thoughts/Actions:

303

"Some stories don't have a clear beginning, middle, and end. Life is about not knowing, having to change, taking the moment and making the best of it, without knowing what's going to happen next. Delicious Ambiguity."

GILDA RADNER

Thoughts/Actions:

304

"Life is like riding a bicycle. To keep your balance you must keep moving."

ALBERT EINSTEIN

Thoughts/Actions:

305

"Accept - then act. Whatever the present moment contains, accept it as if you had chosen it. Always work with it, not against it."

ECKHART TOLLE

Thoughts/Actions:

306

"Learn from the past… then get the heck out of there."

UNKNOWN

Don't allow what's done & over with to hold you back, or take up too much space in your mind - or any space at all. Appreciate what you've learned and keep moving forward.

Thoughts/Actions:

307

"Learn to respect all kinds of people. Because everyone is fighting a battle on their own. We all have our problems, bad sides, and bad days. But there is so much more behind it. Behind me, behind you, behind everyone. "

UNKNOWN

Thoughts/Actions:

308

"Cherish your LIFE. Cherish your HEALTH. Cherish your FAMILY. Cherish your FRIENDS. For these are the things that money can't buy and will define YOUR TRUE WEALTH."

UNKNOWN

Cherish your true wealth. Cherish today.

Thoughts/Actions:

309

"All you need to know and observe in yourself is this: Whenever you feel superior or inferior to anyone, that's the ego in you."

ECKHART TOLLE

Thoughts/Actions:

310

"The world gives our children enough news about tragedy, hopelessness, hate and misery. Let us be the beacons of light to them and share the good news of love, hope, courage, forgiveness, comfort and joy."

CAROLINE NAOROJI

Who wouldn't want this for their children? Be aware of what you're sharing with the children & people around you. Are you focused on, and sharing your worries? Or are you focused on and sharing the good news of love, hope, courage, forgiveness, comfort, and joy?

Thoughts/Actions:

311

STRESS LESS

1. Dance it out
2. Go for a walk
3. Talk about it
4. Breathe
5. Go to bed earlier
6. Focus on what you can control
7. Reminisce about good times
8. Ask for a hug
9. Look for opportunities in life's challenges
10. Smile

UNKNOWN

Which of these can you do right now to move in a less stressful direction? Here's to less stress, and more fun & relaxation.

Thoughts/Actions:

312

8 Ways to Declutter Your Mind

1. Accept what is
2. Be kind to yourself
3. Release your guilt and fears
4. Let go of control
5. Visualize what's important to you
6. Focus on your life-force energy
7. Allow yourself to be vulnerable
8. Find what doesn't serve or interest you and let it go

Thoughts/Actions:

313

"Take control of what you can, let go of what you can't"

UNKNOWN

Thoughts/Actions:

314

"The voice in your head is like a wild horse taking you wherever it wants to go. Once you tame the horse, you can ride the horse, and knowledge becomes a tool for communication that takes you where you want to go."

DON MIGUEL RUIZ

Thoughts/Actions:

315

"At the end of the day, the only questions I will ask myself are... Did I love enough? Did I laugh enough? Did I make a difference?"

KATRINA MAYER

Thoughts/Actions:

316

"Remember, you are the only person who thinks in your mind! You are the power and authority in your world."

LOUISE HAY

Thoughts/Actions:

317

"The real question is not whether life exists after death. The real question is whether you are alive before death."

OSHO

Thoughts/Actions:

318

"There are some people who always seem angry and continuously look for conflict. Walk away; the battle they are fighting isn't with you, it is with themselves."

UNKNOWN

Thoughts/Actions:

319

"Life is really simple but we insist on making it complicated."

CONFUCIUS

Life is simple. Are you happy?
Yes = Keep going
No = Change something

Learn to appreciate "negative" emotions. They are just a guidance system, nothing more, teaching us that we may want to change something or move in another direction. So simple really... It only gets complicated

when we ignore the guidance system within. And have fun with it. When feeling down, be thankful that your guidance system is working for YOU, and then make positive steps in the right direction.

Thoughts/Actions:

320

"If you are happy, happiness will come to you because happiness wants to go where happiness is."

YOGI BHAJAN

Do what makes you happy!

Thoughts/Actions:

321

{Karma Cleanse}

Be grateful
Act with love
Check your motives
Watch your attitude
Forgive

Thoughts/Actions:

322

"Where we put our attention is what we experience--our personal dream."

DON MIGUEL RUIZ

Where are you putting your attention today?

Thoughts/Actions:

323

"Change NOW and accept failures as lessons or accept staying the SAME. Which one hurts more? Stop the blame and excuses and OWN your life."

LORI HARDER

"Change is the essence of life. Be willing to surrender what you are, for what you could become."

UNKNOWN

Thoughts/Actions:

324

"The best predictor of future behavior is past behavior, so you have to create a new history."

DR. PHIL

"It's a choice. You just have to decide that I'm not going to put my energy there. I'm going to decide to let this go. It's your choice. You can embrace it, you can become a prisoner of bitterness and resentment, anger and victim city, or you can just say 'I'm going to live my life and be happy'.

DR. PHIL

Thoughts/Actions:

325

"Never mind what is or what has been. Imagine it the way you want it to be so that your vibration is a match to your desire."

ABRAHAM HICKS

Use your imagination and remember paradise is a state of mind; therefore, life can be a permanent vacation.

Thoughts/Actions:

326

"Today I will judge nothing that occurs."

A COURSE IN MIRACLES

Thoughts/Actions:

327

"The KEY to happiness is letting each situation be what it is instead of what you think it SHOULD be."

MANDY HALE

Thoughts/Actions:

328

"The extra mile is the stretch of the road that is never crowded."

UNKNOWN

Go above and beyond.

Thoughts/Actions:

329

"The reason many people in our society are miserable, sick, and highly stressed is because of an unhealthy attachment to things they have no control over."

STEVE MARABOLI

Thoughts/Actions:

330

"The new paradigm of loving relationships has no drama. Love is at its core. Real and authentic. It does not judge, it does not plead for help, it just is. There is nothing to nurture, nothing to change, nothing to pine for; it will already be in its glorious perfection. This is what you have to look forward to. Being love and being love with each other. Oh, it will be glorious."

MARY SOLIEL AUTHOR OF "MICHAEL'S CLARION CALL"

Thoughts/Actions:

331

20 things to start doing in your relationships

1. Free yourself from negative people
2. Let go of those who are already gone
3. Give people you don't know a fair chance
4. Show everyone kindness and respect
5. Accept people just the way they are
6. Encourage others and cheer for them
7. Be your imperfectly perfect self
8. Forgive people and move forward
9. Do little things every day for others
10. Always be loyal
11. Stay in better touch with people who matter to you
12. Keep your promises and tell the truth
13. Give what you want to receive
14. Say what you mean and mean what you say
15. Allow others to make their own decisions
16. Talk a little less, and listen more
17. Leave petty arguments alone
18. Pay attention to your relationship with yourself
19. Pay attention to who your real friends are
20. Ignore unconstructive, hurtful commentary

UNKNOWN

Thoughts/Actions:

332

"Enjoy today, knowing that some of the best days of your life haven't happened yet."

UNKNOWN

Thoughts/Actions:

333

How you attract with the Law of Attraction:

Your words affect your thoughts
Your thoughts affect your feelings
Your feelings affect your vibration
Your vibration is what attracts things to you

UNKNOWN

Everything is vibrating... "If you want to find the secrets of the Universe, think in terms of energy, frequency and vibration."

NIKOLA TESLA

Raise your vibration! Sing a song, dance, and smile, watch your pet play, recall a fond memory, give, do something nice for someone, watch your favorite movie, etc. Easy right?

Thoughts/Actions:

334

"The Universe is not punishing you or blessing you. The Universe is responding to the vibrational attitude that you are emitting."

ABRAHAM HICKS

Thoughts/Actions:

335

"To know even one life has breathed easier because you have lived, this is to have succeeded."

RALPH WALDO EMERSON

Thoughts/Actions:

336

"Dreams are renewable. No matter what our age or condition, there are still untapped possibilities within us and new beauty waiting to be born."

DALE E. TURNER

"Dreams are illustrations from the book your soul is writing about you."

MARSHA NORMAN

Follow your dreams.... they know the way.

Thoughts/Actions:

337

"If life gives us rocks, don't sit back and blame life for that. At every turn of our life, it gives us choices which we fail to recognize. So when life gives you rocks, it's still your choice whether to build a wall or to build a bridge."

UNKNOWN

Thoughts/Actions:

338

"The older I get, the less I care about what people think of me. Therefore the older I get, the more I enjoy life."

UNKNOWN

Thoughts/Actions:

339

"It helps if you remember that everyone is doing their best from their level of consciousness."

DEEPAK CHOPRA

Thoughts/Actions:

340

Drop and give me ZEN
Drop regrets
Drop limiting beliefs
Drop resentments
Drop doubts
Drop worries

UNKNOWN

"Worrying doesn't take away tomorrow's troubles; it takes away today's peace."

UNKNOWN

Thoughts/Actions:

341

"The strongest factor for success is self-esteem; believing you can do it, believing you deserve it, believing you will get it."

UNKNOWN

Thoughts/Actions:

342

"Put all excuses aside and remember this: You are capable!"

ZIG ZIGLAR

Thoughts/Actions:

343

"Don't just chase your dreams. Stalk them. Hide in the bushes. Follow them around town. If your dreams aren't seriously considering a restraining order against you, get busy!"

UNKNOWN

Thoughts/Actions:

344

"The first step towards getting somewhere is to decide that you are not going to stay where you are."

UNKNOWN

Thoughts/Actions:

345

"Stop hating yourself for everything you aren't. Start loving yourself for everything that you are..."

UNKNOWN

"Why not love ourselves unconditionally? Why spend our lives creating conflict with ourselves by judging ourselves, rejecting ourselves, or living our lives in shame, guilt or blame?"

DON MIGUEL RUIZ

Do you ever feel unnecessary guilt? I was unable to get a good photo of my daughter at her 8th grade graduation... which made me feel sad, frustrated & guilty. This is just one example of how we allow ourselves to feel negative emotions on a regular basis for really no good reason. I also feel guilty when I eat too much chocolate, or bread... the list goes on and on. BUT, if my daughter had been unable to get a good photo, I would've said "That's okay. You tried your best. It's no big deal." And if my daughter ate too much junk food I'd say "I hope you enjoyed that chocolate. Don't allow yourself to feel bad about it. Just learn from your bellyache and start fresh tomorrow." Let's be easier on ourselves. Let's love ourselves enough to let go of the past and the things we cannot change. Once you become aware of negative emotions, then you can go about changing them. Let them go, and replace them with better feeling thoughts. Recall ALL the good in your life, and ALL the good that you are.

Thoughts/Actions:

346

"Put your hand on your heart and just ask yourself internally what kind of world do I want to live in? And now ask yourself how can I make that happen?"

DEEPAK CHOPRA

"There is more good than bad in this world, more light than darkness and YOU can make more light."

PETER H. REYNOLDS

Thoughts/Actions:

347

"It's not what you say out of your mouth that determines your life; it's what you whisper to yourself that has the most power"

ROBERT T. KIYOSAKI

Thoughts/Actions:

348

"Wouldn't it be powerful if you fell in love with yourself so deeply that you would do just about anything if you knew it would make you happy? This is precisely how much life loves you and wants you to nurture yourself. The deeper you love yourself, the more the universe will affirm your worth. Then you can enjoy a lifelong love affair that brings you the richest fulfillment from inside out."

ALAN COHEN

Thoughts/Actions:

349

"Take chances, take a lot of them. Because honestly, no matter where you end up and with whom, it always ends up just the way it should be. Your mistakes make you who you are. You learn and grow with each choice you make. Everything is worth it. Say how you feel, always. Be you, and be okay with it."

UNKNOWN

Thoughts/Actions:

350

"When nobody else celebrates you, learn to celebrate yourself. When nobody else compliments you, then compliment yourself. It's not up to other people to keep you encouraged. It's up to you. Encouragement should come from the inside."

UNKNOWN

Thoughts/Actions:

351

"The most sacred place in the world is your mind. Guard it ferociously."

RICK BENETEAU

Thoughts/Actions:

352

"Failure is only the opportunity to begin again, only this time more wisely."

UNKNOWN

Thoughts/Actions:

353

"Rise in the morning with the spirit you had known in childhood. That spirit of eagerness and adventure and certainty."

UNKNOWN

Thoughts/Actions:

354

"Write out a not-to-do list. Put things on it that kill your productivity and waste your time. Then when you find yourself doing one of those things stop immediately and redirect yourself."

UNKNOWN

Thoughts/Actions:

355

"Do not tell me how hard you work. Tell me how much you get done."

JAMES LING

Thoughts/Actions:

356

"The greatest gift that you were ever given was the gift of your imagination."

WAYNE DYER

"Never mind what is. Imagine it the way you want it to be, so that your vibration is a match to your desire. When your vibration is a match to your desire, all things in your experience will gravitate to meet that match...every time. Your hands are tied in action, but your hands are not tied in imagination and everything springs forth from the imagination. Everything."

ABRAHAM HICKS

Thoughts/Actions:

357

"You live longer once you realize that any time spent being unhappy is wasted."

RUTH E. RENKL

Thoughts/Actions:

358

"You cannot hang out with negative people and expect to live a positive life."

JOEL OSTEEN

Thoughts/Actions:

359

"The greatest gift you can give someone is your TIME. Because when you give your time, you are giving a portion of your life that you will never get back."

UNKNOWN

"Time is free, but it's priceless.
You can't own it, but you can use it.
You can't keep it, but you can spend it.
Once you've lost it, you can never get it back."

HARVEY MACKAY

Thoughts/Actions:

360

"The most important decision you make is to be in a good mood."

VOLTAIRE

Thoughts/Actions:

361

"We must never forget the importance of gratitude. Say THANK YOU when your heart is full, AND when it breaks, and when you are alone and sad, and when you dance with joy and when things are lost and found again. Day and night give thanks for this incredibly beautiful, tragic gift called Life."

SEADREAMSTUDIO.COM

Thoughts/Actions:

362

"Courage is the power to let go of the familiar."

UNKNOWN

Thoughts/Actions:

363

"Reflections we see are simply perceptions we have chosen. There is love and beauty in all of us and everything. Look for love and you will find it."

UNKNOWN

The World Is Your Reflection

There is a story they tell of two dogs…

Both at separate times walk into the same room.

One comes out wagging his tail while the other comes out growling.

A woman watching this goes into the room to see what could possibly make one dog so happy and the other so mad.

To her surprise she finds a room filled with mirrors.

The happy dog found a thousand happy dogs looking back at him while the angry dog found a thousand dogs growling back at him.

What you see in the world around you is a reflection of who you are.

UNKNOWN

Thoughts/Actions:

364

"Let go of your attachment to being right, and suddenly your mind is more open. You're able to benefit from the unique viewpoints of others, without being crippled by your own judgment."

RALPH MARSTON

Thoughts/Actions:

365

LIVE...

"I have forgiven mistakes that were indeed almost unforgivable. I've tried to replace people who were irreplaceable and tried to forget those who were unforgettable. I've acted on impulse; have been disappointed by people when I thought that this could never be possible. But I have also disappointed those who I love. I have laughed at inappropriate occasions. I've made friends that are now friends for life. I've screamed and jumped for joy. I've loved and I've been loved. But I have also been rejected and I have been loved without loving the person back. I've lived for love alone and made vows of eternal love. I've had my heart broken many, many times! I've cried while listening to music and looking at old pictures. I've called someone just to hear their voice on the other side. I have fallen in love with a smile. At times, I thought I would die because I missed someone so much. At other times, I felt very afraid that I might lose someone very special (which ended up happening anyway.) But I have lived! And I still continue living every day. I'm not just passing through life… and you shouldn't either. Live! The best thing in life is to go ahead with all your plans and your dreams, to embrace life and to live everyday with passion, to lose and still keep the faith and to win while being grateful. All of this because the world belongs to those who dare to go after what they want. And because life is really too short to be insignificant."

CHARLIE CHAPLIN

Thoughts/Actions:

Afterword

"You must unlearn what you have been programmed to believe since birth. That software no longer serves you if you want to live in a world where all things are possible."

~ JACQUELINE E. PURCELL

The intention of this book is to keep things simple and to provoke thought and action; to empower you on your journey, and to remind you of your strength. When you make it a habit to incorporate positive changes into your life, one day at a time, you will reap many benefits. Live in the present, and appreciate each day while moving forward towards your dreams and goals... one baby step at a time. We are meant to love, have fun, and dream big!

12 Things Happy People Do Differently

1. Express gratitude
2. Cultivate optimism
3. Avoid over-thinking and social comparison
4. Practice acts of kindness
5. Nurture social relationships
6. Develop strategies for coping
7. Learn to forgive
8. Increase flow experiences
9. Savor life's joys
10. Commit to your goals
11. Practice spirituality
12. Take care of your body

Other titles by Find Your Way Publishing:

- Always Within; Grieving the Loss of Your Infant
- A Quote a Day to Find Your Way: Quotes & Thoughts to Inspire You on Your Journey
- Guaranteed Success for Kindergarten; 50 Easy Things
- You Can Do Today!
- Guaranteed Success for Grade School; 50 Easy Things You Can Do Today!
- The Secret Combination to Middle School; Real Advice from Real Kids, Ideas for Success, and Much More!
- Prank and Pray You Get Away! - Over 60 Fun Jokes to Play on Your Sibling
- I Love You 1000 Times plus Infinity
- I Miss You 1000 Times plus Infinity
- I'm Sorry 1000 Times plus Infinity
- I Love You 1000 Times plus Infinity - Pocket Edition
- I Miss You 1000 Times plus Infinity - Pocket Edition
- I'm Sorry 1000 Times plus Infinity - Pocket Edition
- Congratulations 1000 Times plus Infinity – Pocket Edition

www.findyourwaypublishing.com

About Melissa Eshleman

Melissa Eshleman lives in Maine, and knows firsthand how inspirational quotes can help someone going through personal struggles. In 2001, the author and her husband experienced the death of their infant son, Lucas, which prompted Melissa to quit her full-time job in the corporate world to become a stay-at-home mom to their four children. This was a frightening and life-changing experience for the entire family.

Struggling to make ends meet financially, Melissa realized that there was an infinite amount of value in time spent with loved ones—more than money could ever provide. Melissa eventually found support through an infant loss group online, where she learned about how others had overcome their grief. This is when she discovered the power of words to help people grow and conquer their challenges.

Other titles by Melissa Eshleman:

- *Always Within; Grieving the Loss of Your Infant*
- *A Quote a Day to Find Your Way;*
  Quotes & Thoughts to Inspire You on Your Journey

Disclaimer

The purpose of this book is for entertainment purposes only. The author and Find Your Way Publishing, Inc. shall have neither liability nor responsibility to any person or entity with respect to any loss or damage caused, or alleged to have been caused, directly or indirectly, by the information contained in this book. If you do not wish to be bound by the above, you may return this book along with a copy of the receipt to the publisher for a full refund.

Index

Abraham Hicks, 60, 61, 90, 92, 95, 100, 123, 128, 137
Abraham Lincoln, 103
achievement, 54, 82
actions, 6, 6, 12, 16
adventure, 85, 136
adversity, 44, 50
Agapi Stassinopoulos, 32
Alan Cohen, 134
Albert Einstein, 11, 57, 80, 113
Andrew Cohen, 47
Andrew Schneider, 90
Angelica Valerio, 15
Ann Landers, 26
Anthony Robbins, 96
Apuleius, 83
Aristotle, 10, 81, 90
attention, 2, 72, 92, 122, 126
attitude, 1, 23, 33, 77, 81, 121, 128
authentic, 46, 58, 125
Awakening, 14
Ayya Khema, 56
baby steps, 2
Barney Stinson, 98
Bernard Edmonds, 88
Bernice Johnson Reagon, 58
Bill Cosby, 45
bliss, 19
braveness, 31
Brian Tracy, 16, 39, 73
Brooke Foss Westcott, 37
Bruce Lee, 63, 74, 79, 100
Buddha, 9
career, 1
Carlos Castenada, 42
Caroline Naoroji, 116
challenges, 5, 58, 59, 73, 117
change, 5, 4, 20, 28, 42, 65, 67, 76, 90, 91, 102, 110, 111, 113, 120, 125, 132
changes, 18, 42, 109
character, 45, 61, 87, 97

Charles B. Handy, 40
Charles Bukowski, 101
Charles Buxton, 112
Charles F. Kettering, 96
choices, 61, 129
Chris Bradford, 44
Christian Nestell Bovee, 38
Chuck Palahniuk, 86
C. JoyBell C, 41
commitment, 9
compromise, 14, 40, 97
confidence, 9, 93, 104
Confucius, 13, 78, 120
consequences, 34
control, 15, 19, 20, 50, 60, 117, 118, 125
courage, 9, 31, 57, 72, 87, 88, 116
Criss Jami, 31
C.S. Lewis, 51
Cyle Parker, 111
Dalai Lama, 57, 89
Dale E. Turner, 128
Daniel Duane, 85
Daniel Johnson, 109
Dave Pelzer, 43
David Emerald, 2, 109
Dean Koontz, 53
Deepak Chopra, 5, 20, 48, 129, 133
depression, 56
despair, 26, 31, 35, 93
Dietrich Bonhoeffer, 37
difficulties, 9, 14
don Miguel Ruiz, 119, 122, 132
Dorothy Thompson, 99
doubts, 12, 35, 40, 91, 130
dream, 16, 39, 51, 70, 88, 90, 102, 122
Dream Hampton, 7, 53
Dr. Lissa Rankin, 32
Dr. Phil, 123
Eckhart Tolle, 68, 114, 116
Edmund Lee, 108
ego, 19, 46, 116
Elbert Hubbard, 49, 51

Eleanor Roosevelt, 26, 66
Elizabeth I Tudor, 46
Ella Fitzgerald, 42
Emmanuel Teney, 15
Emotions, 15
Eric Roth, 33
Erika Harris, 13
Ernest Hemingway, 22
Excellence, 81
extraordinary, 23, 81
Ezra T. Benson, 7
Failure, 11, 135
faith, 5, 9, 13, 15, 40, 56, 61, 141
flow, 15
Focus, 6, 48, 106, 117, 118
forgive, 4, 11, 25, 45
Forgive, 5, 121, 126
forgiveness, 31, 70, 116
Forgiveness, 11, 65
forgives, 5
Frans Johansson, 88
Frederick William Robertson, 44
free, 3, 4, 13, 20, 95, 101, 138
Gene Wolfe, 105
George Bernard Shaw, 83
George Washington Carver, 22
Gilda Radner, 113
goals, 85, 111
Greatness, 10
guidance, 120
guilt, 118, 132
Guru Eduardo, 16
habit, 13, 81
happiness, 49, 121, 124
happy, 20, 30, 49, 60, 66, 72, 106, 120,
    121, 123, 134, 140
Harvey Mackay, 138
H.E. Davey, 56
Helen Keller, 36, 85
Henry David Thoreau, 73
Henry Miller, 94
Henry Rollins, 97
Henry Ward Beecher, 10, 38
higher purpose, 87
Humility, 7
humor, 45, 65

Hunter S. Thompson, 89
imagination, 20, 123, 137
infinite, 17, 92
inspire, 5, 6, 16
Jack Kornfield, 14
Jaime Buckley, 60
James Allen, 36
James Freeman Clarke, 40
James Ling, 136
James Naismith, 38
Jason Randal, 88
J.D. Stroube, 31
Jean Claude Van Damme, 99
Jennifer Armintrout, 34
Jennifer Gayle, 106, 110
Jenny G. Perry, 3
Jerry Rice, 76
Joel Osteen, 138
John C. Maxwell, 12
John F Kennedy, 9
John O'Donohue, 40
John Quincy Adams, 16
Josefa Iloilo, 83
Joseph Addison, 8
Joss Whedon, 28, 46
joy, 20, 116, 139, 141
judgments, 15
Katherine Mansfield, 34
Katrina Mayer, 119
Ken Keyes, 10
Knute Rockne, 37
Lao Tzu, 12, 24
Lauryn Hill, 22
Lawrence G. Lovasik, 45
leader, 16
Leo Buscaglia, 2
let go, 19, 26, 118, 132, 139
Lewis Carroll, 96
limitations, 77
Lisa Villa Prosen, 58
Lori Harder, 122
Louisa May Alcott, 12
Louise Carey, 28
Louise Erdrich, 21

love, 4, 21, 24, 47, 51, 59, 61, 62, 65, 70, 75, 92, 102, 116, 119, 121, 125, 132, 134, 139, 141
loving, 10, 125, 132, 141
Lt. Cmdr. Greitens, 87
luck, 21
Mahatma Gandhi, 11, 20, 28, 52
Mandy Hale, 124
Manny Pacquiao, 73
Marcus Aurelius, 25
Margaret Thatcher, 97, 99
Marisa Stein, 30
Mark Twain, 84, 111
Marsha Norman, 128
Martha Graham, 44
Marvin J. Aston, 59
Mary Gaohlee Thao, 27
Mary Oliver, 41
Mary Soliel, 125
May Sarton, 35
Michael Bernard Beckwith, 72
Michael J. Fox, 30
Michael Jordan, 1, 33, 75, 79
Michael P. Watson, 61
Michael Sotelo, 26
mistakes, 12, 32, 43, 57, 63, 68, 70, 134, 141
Mitch Albom, 54
Muhammad Ali, 76, 77
Myles Munroe, 95
Napoleon Hill, 36, 81
negativity, 56, 62
new day, 6, 26
Nikola Tesla, 127
Norman Vincent Peale, 9, 13
obstacle, 43
obstacles, 23
Og Mandino, 11, 93
Oliver Wendell Holmes, 19
opportunities, 23, 100, 102, 117
opportunity, 17, 60, 63, 64, 135
opposition, 11
optimism, 9
Orison Swett Marden, 23, 24, 58
Osho, 3, 120
pain, 4, 31, 35, 48, 57, 78, 87

passion, 58, 102, 141
Patricia Neal, 23
Paulo Coelho, 31, 48
P.C. Cast, 35
peace, 52, 105, 130
Peace, 72
perseverance, 13, 23, 38
persistence, 9, 23
Peter H. Reynolds, 133
Peter Singer, 104
Plato, 101
positive, 5, 3, 23, 42, 64, 71, 81, 121, 138
potential, 6, 3, 39, 42, 54, 55, 56, 60, 75, 76, 90, 91, 93, 94
pray, 5, 9, 79
prayer, 9, 44
Pride, 7, 80
Rainer Maria Rilke, 47
Ralph Marston, 140
Ralph Waldo Emerson, 21, 54, 59, 128
Respect, 66
responsibility, 91, 149
Richard J. Needham, 43
Richard M. Nixon, 100
Rick Beneteau, 135
Risk, 34
Robert T. Kiyosaki, 133
Rocky Balboa, 98
Rollo May, 103
Ronald Osborn, 83
Rosalia de Castro, 7
Rosalynn Carter, 104
Ruth E. Renkl, 137
Sahih al-Bukhari, 29
Sarah Dessen, 25
Security, 85
self-esteem, 92, 93, 99, 109, 130
silence, 27
soul, 5, 23, 39, 94, 101, 128
Spiritual Growth, 18
Sri Chinmoy, 104
Steve House, 86
Steve Maraboli, 4, 29, 42, 53, 91, 94, 125
Steven Redhead, 93

strength, 5, 9, 10, 13, 25, 26, 31, 33, 35, 40, 44, 45, 46, 47, 48, 59, 71, 79, 87, 88, 103, 105

Strength, 28, 29, 34, 45, 79

strengths, 6

strong, 5, 2, 10, 11, 12, 22, 23, 24, 25, 29, 31, 36, 37, 38, 40, 42, 43, 44, 48, 49, 50, 51, 52, 57, 59, 62, 78, 82, 99, 100, 104, 105

struggles, 30

Sydney J. Harris, 55

T.F. Hodge, 105

Thema Davis, 112

Theodore Roosevelt, 82

Thomas Carlyle, 23, 43

Thomas Jefferson, 77

Thomas Paine, 47, 95

time, 3, 4, 5, 7, 13, 15, 20, 24, 48, 53, 71, 78, 94, 97, 102, 106, 110, 112, 135, 136, 137, 138

Time, 3, 138

Toba Beta, 55

tolerance, 59

Tony Gaskins, 63, 70

trust, 4, 5, 9, 15, 30, 88

truth, 34, 42, 51, 56, 126

T.S. Eliot, 84

Ursula K. Le Guin, 45

vibration, 19, 123, 127, 137

victim, 24, 89, 91, 123

Victoria Addino, 105

Viktor E. Frankl, 1

visualize, 20

Voltaire, 138

Wayne Dyer, 72, 137

Wayne Gerard Trotman, 93

weakness, 33, 45

William Faulkner, 39

William Shakespeare, 5

William Wordsworth, 29

Will Rogers, 3

Winston Churchill, 85

wisdom, 44

Yip Harburg, 97

yogi bhajan, 121

Yvon Chouinard, 101

Zig Ziglar, 61, 131

It's Never too Late to Navigate

365 Quotes to a Better You

Quick Order Form

Fax orders:
207-514-0438.
Please send this form with your order.

Telephone orders:
207-514-0575

Internet orders:
www.findyourwaypublishing.com

Postal orders:
Find Your Way Publishing, Inc.
PO Box 667
Norway, ME 04268
USA

Please include:
  Name of book:
  Quantity:
  Your Name:
  Address:
  City:
  State:
  Zip:
  Telephone:
  Email address:

www.ingramcontent.com/pod-product-compliance
Lightning Source LLC
LaVergne TN
LVHW011236080426
835509LV00005B/519